CIEL PUBLISHING

VALENTINE'S DAY JOKE BOOK

AGES 5-12

FOR KIDS

Why Did Cupid Cross the Road?

Why did the clock's date cancel their Valentine's Day dinner?

Because he tocked too much.

TABLE OF CONTENTS

INTRODUCTION

Get ready to spread some love and laughter with our Valentine's Day Joke Book for Kids!

Inside you'll find a collection of silly, sweet and playful jokes that are perfect for sharing with friends and family on Valentine's Day. This book is filled with a variety of jokes that will have everyone chuckling. Whether you're looking for a fun way to brighten up a class party or just want to make your loved ones smile, this book is sure to bring joy to your Valentine's Day celebrations.

So grab a friend, grab a smile, and get ready for some Valentine's Day fun!

CHAPTER 1
Knock, Knock! It's Valentine's Day Joke Time!

Knock, knock!

Who's there?

Will.

Will who?

Will you be my Valentine?

Knock, knock!

Who's there?

Luke.

Luke who?

Luke who just got a Valentine!

Knock, knock!

Who's there?

Jamaica.

Jamaica who?

Jamaica great Valentine.

Knock, knock!

Who's there?

Bea.

Bea who?

Bea my Valentine!

Knock, knock!

Who's there?

Abby.

Abby who?

Abby Valentine's Day!

Knock, knock!

Who's there?

Honeydew.

Honeydew who?

Honeydew you know how much I love you?

❤ - - ❤ - - ❤ - - ❤ - - ❤ - →

Knock, knock!

Who's there?

Dough.

Dough who?

Dough you want to be my Valentine?

Knock, knock!

Who's there?

Wanda.

Wanda who?

Wanda be my Valentine?

Knock, knock!

Who's there?

Tom.

Tom who?

Tom-orrow is Valentine's Day!

Knock, knock!

Who's there?

Egg.

Egg who?

Egg-cited to be your Valentine.

❤--❤--❤--❤--❤--▶

Knock, knock!

Who's there?

Weekend.

Weekend who?

Weekend do anything we want
this Valentine's Day!

Knock, knock!

Who's there?

Bee.

Bee who?

Bee my Valentine!

❤--❤--❤--❤--❤--▶

Knock, knock!

Who's there?

Olive.

Olive who?

Olive you and want to be your Valentine!

Knock, knock!

Who's there?

Lettuce.

Lettuce who?

Lettuce be each other's Valentines!

Knock, knock!

Who's there?

Adore.

Adore who?

Adore you, of course!

CHAPTER 2
School's Out for Valentine's Day Fun!

Why did the clock cancel its Valentine's dinner?

It was too stressed and needed time to unwind.

❤ - - ❤ - - ❤ - - ❤ - - ❤ - →

What did the math book say to the pencil on Valentine's Day?

"You complete me!"

What did the math teacher say to the students on Valentine's Day?

"I love you all equally."

❤ - - ❤ - - ❤ - - ❤ - - ❤ - - ▶

What did the notebook say to the pen on Valentine's Day?

"Without you, I'd be empty."

❤ - - ❤ - - ❤ - - ❤ - - ❤ - - ▶

What's a laptop's favorite snack to share on Valentine's Day?

Computer chips.

❤ - - ❤ - - ❤ - - ❤ - - ❤ - - ▶

Why did the computer have to cancel her Valentine's Day date?

Because she had a virus.

Where can you easily find a Valentine's Day date?

On the calendar.

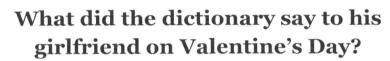

What did the dictionary say to his girlfriend on Valentine's Day?

"You really add meaning to my life."

Why was the calendar sad on Valentine's Day?

Because it had no dates!

Why couldn't the paper plane get to his Valentine's date?

Because he was stationary.

How did the English teacher write her Valentine a love note?

She used big words to express her love.

Why didn't the triangle ask the circle out on a Valentine's date?

Because it was pointless.

Where did the tulip take his date on Valentine's Day?

He took her to kinder-garden.

Why was the English book sad on Valentine's Day?

Because it had too many tragic stories.

Where does the stationary love to go on Valentine's Day?

Pennsylvania.

How did the keyboard ask the mouse on a Valentine's date?

"You're just my type, will you go out with me?"

What do you call cheese that's sad on Valentine's Day?

Blue cheese.

❤ - - ❤ - - ❤ - - ❤ - - ❤ - - ▶

What did the magnet say to the paperclip?

"I'm really attracted to you."

❤ - - ❤ - - ❤ - - ❤ - - ❤ - - ▶

What did the glue say to the paper on Valentine's Day?

"I will always stick with you."

What did the calculator say to the math book on Valentine's Day?

"You're the reason I exist."

What did the coloring book say to the crayons on Valentine's Day?"

"You bring color to my life."

What did the computer say when delivering his Valentine's Day card?

"Tell my Wi-fi love her."

Why was the geography book sad on Valentine's Day?

It didn't know where in the world to find love.

Why was the science book feeling left out on Valentine's Day?

Because it didn't have any chemistry with the other books!

What did the calculator say to the pen?

"You can count on me."

Why was the math book feeling happy on Valentine's Day?

Because it was solving love equations all day long!

CHAPTER 3
Yum! It's Valentine's Food Jokes!

Why couldn't the cucumber attend his Valentine's Day dinner?

Because he was in a pickle.

❤--❤--❤--❤--❤--▶

Why was the tomato blushing on Valentine's Day?

Because it saw the salad dressing!

What did the beet say to his girlfriend on Valentine's Day?

"You make my heart beet really fast."

What did the pickle say when she broke up with her Valentine?

"Dill with it."

What did the one mushroom say to the other after their Valentine's date?

"You're a really fungi."

What did the one plate say to the other on Valentine's Day?

"Dinner is on me!"

Why was the strawberry sad on Valentine's Day?

Because her date was in a jam.

Why did the walnut tell jokes all night on Valentine's Day?

He wanted to crack up his date.

What do pumpkins love to do on Valentine's Day?

They love to play squash.

What did the chocolate say to the Valentine?

"You're looking so sweet today."

❤ - - ❤ - - ❤ - - ❤ - - ❤ - -▶

Why couldn't the bread go on a date on Valentine's Day?

Because it kneaded to rest.

❤ - - ❤ - - ❤ - - ❤ - - ❤ - -▶

How did the pineapple answer the phone when her Valentine called?

"Yellow?"

❤ - - ❤ - - ❤ - - ❤ - - ❤ - -▶

What did the glue say to the Valentine's Day card?

"Stick with me, and I will take you places!"

What did the watermelon say to his date on Valentine's Day?

"You really are one in a Melon."

What did one slice of toast say to the other slice?

"You are definitely my butter half!"

Why didn't the potatoes go out on Valentine's Day?

Because it was on Fry-day.

Why did the biscuit go to the doctor on Valentine's Day?

Because it was feeling crumby.

What did the coffee bean say when his girlfriend canceled their Valentine's Day plans?

"How do you sleep at night?!"

What did the girl say when her boyfriend tried to eat from her plate on Valentine's Day?

"Hey! This is nacho cheese!"

What did the bread do on Valentine's Day?

Not much; they love to loaf around.

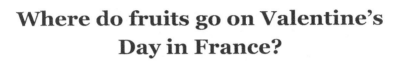

Where do fruits go on Valentine's Day in France?

They go to Pear-is.

Where did the kittens go on Valentine's Day?

To the mew-seum.

Why did the banana split on Valentine's Day?

Because it saw the apple dumpling!

What did the spaghetti say to its Valentine?

"I'm a noodle in love."

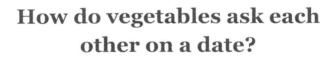

How do vegetables ask each other on a date?

"Peas would you be my Valentine."

Why did the flower ask a few flowers to be his Valentine?

He was just looking for some-buddy to love.

What do chefs give their wives for Valentine's Day?

They give them a hug and a quiche.

What did the vegetable say to its Valentine's Day date?

"I love you from my head to-ma-toes."

What did the honey say to the bee on Valentine's Day?

"You are the bee's knees!"

What did the cherry write on his Valentine's Day card?

"In case I haven't told you, I love you berry, berry much."

How do coffees express their love for each other on Valentine's Day?

"Words can't espresso how much I love you."

❤ - - ❤ - - ❤ - - ❤ - - ❤ ➤

How did the loaf of bread tell his Valentine how he felt about her?

"You're the love of my life."

❤ - - ❤ - - ❤ - - ❤ - - ❤ - - ➤

What did the candy say to her boyfriend on Valentine's Day?

"I think we were mint to be together."

❤ - - ❤ - - ❤ - - ❤ - - ❤ - - ➤

What's a vegetable's favorite kind of Valentine's Day joke?

A corny joke.

What did the turnip drink on its Valentine's Day date?

A root beer.

How do cheeses ask each other out on Valentine's Day?

"Will you Brie mine?"

How do desserts express their love on Valentine's Day?

"I donut what I would do without you in my life."

What did the banana buy his girlfriend for Valentine's Day?

A pair of slippers.

❤ - - ❤ - - ❤ - - ❤ - - ❤ - - ➤

What food did the cats order on Valentine's Day?

Purrr-itos.

❤ - - ❤ - - ❤ - - ❤ - - ❤ - - ➤

Why did the chocolate go on a date with the ice cream on Valentine's Day?

Because it was feeling scoop-er in love.

❤ - - ❤ - - ❤ - - ❤ - - ❤ - - ➤

Why did the vegetarian break up with her boyfriend on Valentine's Day?

She realized dating him with a huge mi-steak.

What did the almond say to its Valentine?

"I have to admit; I'm nuts about you!"

Why did the bee give his girlfriend a heart-shaped box of chocolates on Valentine's Day?

Because he's a honey!

What did the bread say to its Valentine?

"I am bread over heels for you."

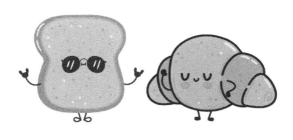

❤ - - ❤ - - ❤ - - ❤ - - ❤ - - ▶

What did one Mars bar say to the other who arrived long past their date time?

"You are choco-late."

CHAPTER 4
Fur-bulous Valentine's Day Jokes

Why couldn't the snake ask his girlfriend on a Valentine's Day date?

Because he was hiss-terical with nerves.

♥--♥--♥--♥--♥--▶

How did the Orca ask his girlfriend on a date?

"Whale you be my Valentine?"

Why couldn't the leopard surprise his girlfriend on Valentine's Day?

"Because he was always spotted."

What type of dog did Dracula get his girlfriend for Valentine's Day?

He got a bloodhound.

What did the elephant say to his date on Valentine's Day?

"I love you a ton!"

How did the bee get ready for her Valentine's Day date?

By honey-combing her hair.

What did the Dalmatian say after eating his Valentine's dinner?

"Thanks, that really hit the spot."

❤--❤--❤--❤--❤--▶

How did the spider choose a restaurant to visit on Valentine's Day?

He checked on the web.

❤--❤--❤--❤--❤--▶

What did the porcupine say when her Valentine kissed her?

"Ouch!"

How did the fish ask his girlfriend to a Valentine's Day dinner?

He dropped her a line.

❤ - - ❤ - - ❤ - - ❤ - - ❤ - - ➤

What sports do bees love to play on Valentine's Day?

They love to play rug-bee.

❤ - - ❤ - - ❤ - - ❤ - - ❤ - - ➤

What did the butterflies say to his Valentine's Day date?

"You give me humans in my tummy."

❤ - - ❤ - - ❤ - - ❤ - - ❤ - - ➤

What is a cat's favorite flowers to receive on Valentine's Day?

Purrrr-ple flowers.

Why did the two dogs stay home on Valentine's Day?

Because it was just puppy love.

❤ - - ❤ - - ❤ - - ❤ - - ❤ - - ➤

Why didn't the shrimp share his dessert with his Valentine's date?

Because he was too shellfish.

❤ - - ❤ - - ❤ - - ❤ - - ❤ - - ➤

Where did the sheep take his girlfriend on Valentine's Day?

He took her to the baaa-hamas.

❤ - - ❤ - - ❤ - - ❤ - - ❤ - - ➤

What do you call two doves who just got married?

Lovebirds.

What are insects called when they're dating?

Lovebugs.

How did the bunnies get to their Valentine's Day dinner?

They took a hare-plane.

Why were the wolves so happy after their Valentine's Day date?

Because it was a howling success.

How did the cat bake a cake for his Valentine?

He baked it from scratch.

Why was the rabbit so happy on Valentine's Day?

Because Somebunny sent her flowers!

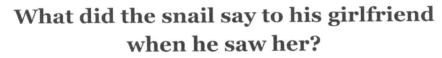

What did the snail say to his girlfriend when he saw her?

"I want to be your Valen-slime."

Why did the birds fly to their Valentine's dinner?

Because it was faster than walking.

What did the cats have for breakfast on Valentine's Day?

They had mice crispies.

Why did the Dolphin flip out of the ocean on Valentine's Day?

Because he was in a fin-tastic mood!

What did the bear say to his Valentine?

"I love you beary much!"

Why did the bird give his girlfriend a box of chocolates on Valentine's Day?

Because he wanted to tweet her something special.

How did the lobster spoil his girlfriend on a Valentine's Day date?

He took her on a shell-icopter ride.

Where did the cows go for their Valentine's Day date?

To the moo-vies.

What takeout do frogs love to order on Valentine's Day?

French-flies.

What movie did the spaghetti take his date to see on Valentine's Day?

To watch mission Impasta-ble.

How do African animals express their love on Valentine's Day?

"I ain't lion when I say I love you."

❤ - - ❤ - - ❤ - - ❤ - - ❤ - - ➤

Why didn't the rooster give his girlfriend anything on Valentine's Day?

Because he was too chicken!

❤ - - ❤ - - ❤ - - ❤ - - ❤ - - ➤

Why couldn't the dog dance with her boyfriend on Valentine's Day?

Because she had two left feet.

Why did the pup cancel her Valentine's Day date?

Because he was feeling a bit ruff.

How do rabbits express their love for each other on Valentine's Day?

"No bunny compares to you."

What did the owl say to his Valentine when she asked him out?

"Owl be yours!"

What did the squirrel say to his Valentine?

"I'm nuts about you!"

Why did the cows have a picnic date on Valentine's Day?

So they could watch the Milky Way.

How did the polar bear ask his girlfriend out on Valentine's Day?"

"I can't bear to be without you."

Where do birds love to go on Valentine's Day?

They go to Swan Lake.

How did the octopus wake his girlfriend on Valentine's Day?

With coffee and ten-tickles.

What did the one shellfish say to the other on Valentine's Day?

"I like your mussels."

❤--❤--❤--❤--❤--▶

What did the labrador say to the other when he tried to ask her on a date?

"You're barking up the wrong tree!"

❤--❤--❤--❤--❤--▶

Why did the mouse give his girlfriend a rose on Valentine's Day?

Because he wanted to show her how much he mouse-t love her, even if it was a little cheesy!

What did the T-rex say when his girlfriend broke up with him on Valentine's Day?

"Now my heart is Dino-sore."

What did the buck say when her Valentine brought flowers to her house?

"You're such a deer; I love you so much."

CHAPTER 5
Valentine's Jokes Are a Full-Time Job

What did the teacher say to her boyfriend when he bought her Valentine's Day flower?

"You get an A+ for effort!"

❤- -❤- -❤- -❤- -❤- -▶

What did the astronaut say to his girlfriend on Valentine's Day?

"I love you to the moon and back."

What did the lawyer say when his Valentine wanted to cancel?

"I object to being alone today!"

What did the baker write in his Valentine's Day card?

"I really knead you in my life."

How did the scientists keep his breath fresh for his Valentine?

With experi-mints.

What did the plumber say to his Valentine when he saw her?

"Are you nervous? You look a bit flushed."

How did the chef show his Valentine's Day date how much he loved her?

He whisked her off her feet!

Why was the janitor late for his Valentine's dinner?

Because he over-swept.

Why couldn't the vampire attend her Valentine's dinner?

Because she was still ill and still coffin.

Where did the ghost take his girlfriend on Valentine's Day?

To the beach for some iScream.

Why did the Pilot cancel his Valentine's Date?

Their love just couldn't take off.

Why did the helium balloon cancel her date with her Valentine?

She refused to be spoken to in that tone.

Why did the scientists have such a great Valentine's date?

Because they had great chemistry.

How did the artist tell his Valentine he loves her?

"I need you more than a painting loves paint."

❤ - - ❤ - - ❤ - - ❤ - - ❤ - - ▶

What kind of dog did the magician buy his girlfriend for Valentine's Day?

He bought a labra-cadabrador.

❤ - - ❤ - - ❤ - - ❤ - - ❤ - - ▶

Why couldn't the chef ask his girlfriend on a Valentine's Day date?

Because she was too spicy for him.

❤ - - ❤ - - ❤ - - ❤ - - ❤ - - ▶

Why couldn't the baker date an athlete?

Because he wanted to be the only breadwinner.

What did the ghost wash his hair with for his Valentine's dinner?

With sham-boo.

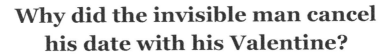

Why did the invisible man cancel his date with his Valentine?

He just couldn't see himself going.

Why did the banana go to the doctor on Valentine's Day?

Because he wasn't peeling well.

What did the lawyer wear to his Valentine's Date?

He wore a lawsuit.

What car did the farmers drive to their Valentine's dinner?

A drove a convertible.

Why did Santa Claus work in the garden on Valentine's Day?

Because he wanted to hoe, hoe, hoe!

Why didn't the nurse go out on Valentine's Day?

She just didn't have the patients for it.

How did the hairdresser get to her Valentine's Day date quickly?

She took a short cut.

How did the surfer greet her boyfriend on Valentine's Day?

She waved excitedly.

Why did the skeleton stay at home on Valentine's Day?

Because he was just a bag of lazy bones.

Why did the mechanic take his girlfriend away for a romantic Valentine's weekend?

Because he wanted to jumpstart their love.

What did the one shellfish say to the other on Valentine's Day?

"I like your mussels."

Why couldn't the keyboard make it to his Valentine's Day dinner?

He had to work an extra shift.

Why did the electrician give his girlfriend a lightbulb on Valentine's Day?

Because he wanted to brighten up her day.

Why did the mechanics take the elevator to the restaurant on Valentine's Day?

Because they work on so many levels.

Why did the heart surgeon break up with his girlfriend before Valentine's Day?

The relationship was just too much heart work.

Why did the astronaut take his girlfriend on a Valentine's Day date to outer space?

Because he thought she was out of this world.

What did the rose say when her Valentine canceled their dinner date?

"Oh no! I'm all dressed up with nowhere to grow!"

What was the lawyer's Valentine's name?

Sue.

❤--❤--❤--❤--❤--▶

Why couldn't the vampire get anyone to go out with him on Valentine's Day?

Because everyone said he was a pain in the neck.

❤--❤--❤--❤--❤--▶

Why did the dog-washer cancel his Valentine's dinner?

His map sent him driving in circles. He couldn't make heads or tails of it.

CHAPTER 6
Stay Cozy With These Valentine's Day Jokes

What did the volcano say to his date on Valentine's Day?

"I lava you."

What did the tornado say to his Valentine's Day date?

"Do you want to go for a spin?"

What did the rain wear on his Valentine's Day date?

A wore a rainbow.

❤--❤--❤--❤--❤--▶

Why didn't the mice go out on Valentine's Day?

Because it was raining cats and dogs.

❤--❤--❤--❤--❤--▶

Why was the weatherman feeling particularly happy on Valentine's Day?

Because the forecast was
100% chance of a date.

What did the flame say to his girlfriend on Valentine's Day?

"You make me feel warm and fuzzy."

Why did the wind blow extra hard on Valentine's Day?

Because he wanted to sweep his date off her feet.

Why did the storm clear up on Valentine's Day?

It wanted to create a romantic atmosphere.

Why did the lightning flash more on Valentine's Day?

To add some spark.

What did the snowman say to his girlfriend on Valentine's Day?

"You make me snow happy!"

What happens when two clouds fight on Valentine's Day?

They storm out on each other.

Where did the thunder take his date on Valentine's Day?

He took her to cloud 9.

What did the snowman say to the sun on Valentine's Day?

"You melt my heart!"

What did the star write to his girlfriend on Valentine's Day?

"I love you to the moon and back."

❤ - - ❤ - - ❤ - - ❤ - - ❤ - - ►

Why did the sharks stay home when it snowed on Valentine's Day?

They were scared of getting frostbite.

❤ - - ❤ - - ❤ - - ❤ - - ❤ - - ►

What did the candle say to the match on Valentine's Day?

"You light up my life!"

❤ - - ❤ - - ❤ - - ❤ - - ❤ - - ►

Why did the sun send the cloud flowers on Valentine's Day?

To brighten up its day!

Why couldn't the air go for dinner on Valentine's Day?

Because it made him windy.

❤ - - ❤ - - ❤ - - ❤ - - ❤ - ➤

Why couldn't the trees go swimming on Valentine's Day?

Because they had no swimming trunks.

❤ - - ❤ - - ❤ - - ❤ - - ❤ - ➤

What did lightning bolt say when he saw his girlfriend on Valentine's Day?

"You're shockingly beautiful."

What did the tree say to his Valentine?

"I'm so in leaf with you."

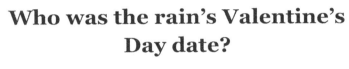

Who was the rain's Valentine's Day date?

Misty.

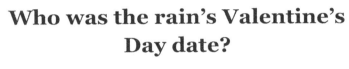

What did the snowman make his girlfriend for breakfast on Valentine's Day?

Snowflakes.

Where did the snowman save up money for his Valentine's Day plans?

In the snow banks.

What did the snowflake say to the other on Valentine's Day?

"I think you're really cool."

CHAPTER 7
Score Big With These Valentine's Day Jokes

Why did the tennis player stay on the court for Valentine's Day?

Because he was looking for his perfect match.

❤ - - ❤ - - ❤ - - ❤ - - ❤ - - ▶

What did the elf want to do on Valentine's Day?

He wanted to play mini-golf.

What did the lions say before having their Valentine's Day meal?

"Let us prey."

❤ – – ❤ – – ❤ – – ❤ – – ❤ – – ▶

Why did the hamburger go to the gym before her Valentine's Date?

She wanted better buns.

❤ – – ❤ – – ❤ – – ❤ – – ❤ – – ▶

What workout did the ghost do before his Valentine's date?

Dead-lifts.

❤ – – ❤ – – ❤ – – ❤ – – ❤ – – ▶

What did the tennis ball say to the other after Valentine's Day?

"See you round."

Where did the tennis players go for Valentine's Day?

To a tennis ball.

❤ - - ❤ - - ❤ - - ❤ - - ❤ - - ➤

Why did the golfer wear two pairs of pants to his Valentine's Day date?

In case he got a hole-in-one.

❤ - - ❤ - - ❤ - - ❤ - - ❤ - - ➤

What did the baseball player say to his date after Valentine's Day?

"Catch ya later!"

Why didn't the grasshoppers watch football on Valentine's Day?

Because they preferred cricket.

What did the cheerleaders have for breakfast on Valentine's Day?

She had Cheerios.

Why did the hockey player take his girlfriend to his game on Valentine's Day?

Because he wanted to break the ice.

What did the soccer player say to his date on Valentine's Day?

"You're a keeper!"

What drinks did the boxers have on Valentine's Day?

Fruit Punch.

❤ - - ❤ - - ❤ - - ❤ - - ❤ - - ▶

What is a soccer player's favorite Valentine's Day beverage?

A penal-tea.

❤ - - ❤ - - ❤ - - ❤ - - ❤ - - ▶

Why did the football player go to the bank on Valentine's Day?

Because he wanted to get his quarterback.

❤ - - ❤ - - ❤ - - ❤ - - ❤ - - ▶

Which animals love to watch sports games on Valentine's Day?

Bats!

Why did the bodybuilders take beers to the gym on Valentine's Day?

They wanted a six-pack.

❤--❤--❤--❤--❤--▶

Why did the ghosts go to the gym on Valentine's Day?

They love to exorcize.

❤--❤--❤--❤--❤--▶

Why did the yoga instructor cancel her dinner on Valentine's Day?

She felt she was always bending over backward.

❤--❤--❤--❤--❤--▶

Why did the gym owner cancel his Valentine's date when she was late?

He just couldn't weight any longer.

Why did the pirate take his girlfriend to the gym on Valentine's Day?

His favorite workout was the plank.

❤--❤--❤--❤--❤--➤

Why did the banana take his date to a gymnastics class on Valentine's Day?

He wanted to show her how to do
a banana split.

❤--❤--❤--❤--❤--➤

Why did the Prince not take Cinderella to a sports game for Valentine's Day?

Because she has a habit of running away
from the ball.

Why didn't the treadmills go on a Valentine's Date?

They knew they'd get nowhere.

The jump rope wanted to go out for Valentine's Day.

But he just ended up skipping it.

What did the boxer's girlfriend say when he told her he wanted to do a workout on Valentine's Day?

"Knock yourself out!"

Why didn't the teddy bear go to the gym before his Valentine's date?

He didn't want to get ripped.

❤--❤--❤--❤--❤--▶

Why did the ghost go to the gym when his Valentine canceled on him?

Because he wanted to lift his spirits.

❤--❤--❤--❤--❤--▶

Why did the dictionary go to the gym before his Valentine's dinner?

Because he wanted to get some definition.

❤--❤--❤--❤--❤--▶

How did the yoga instructor ask his girlfriend to be his Valentine?

"Will you namaste with me?"

Why did the gym guys break up with their girlfriends on Valentine's Day?

Because it just wasn't working out.

❤--❤--❤--❤--❤--▸

Why did the chicken go to the gym before his Valentine's Date?

He wanted to work on his pecks.

❤--❤--❤--❤--❤--▸

Why didn't the yoga instructor go to her Valentine's Day dinner?

The timing wouldn't work—it was quite a stretch.

CHAPTER 8

Plant Some Laughter With These Valentine's Day Jokes

What's inside a flower's favorite Valentine's Day letter?

"Every Daisy is better because of you."

❤ – – ❤ – – ❤ – – ❤ – – ❤ – – ▶

What did the flower say to her boyfriend on Valentine's Day?

"I love you a Lily more every day."

Where did the tree hide his Valentine's Day gift?

In his trunk.

What happened when the flower saw her Valentine for the first time?

She turned rosey.

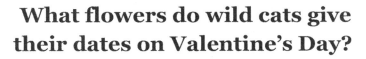

What flowers do wild cats give their dates on Valentine's Day?

Dande-lions.

What did the girl say when her Valentine bought her the wrong flowers?

"Oopsie Daisy!"

Why did the bush go to the barber before his Valentine's date?

Because he needed a trim.

What did the pepper plant write in his Valentine's letter?

"You're the spice of my life!"

Why did the rose cancel her Valentine's Date?

Because she needed time to relax and leaf it all behind.

What did the oak tree say to the maple tree on Valentine's Day?

"You're the leaf of my heart."

What did the pine tree say to his girlfriend?

"You're the pine-apple of my eye."

What did the acorn tree say to the other on Valentine's Day?

"I will never leaf you."

Why did the pepper wear a jacket on Valentine's Day?

He was chili.

What did the beetroot say to her girlfriend on Valentine's Day?

"You make my heart skip a beet."

What did the desert plants say to each other on Valentine's Day?

"Aloe you vera much."

How did the tree ask the other tree to be his Valentine?

"Wood you be mine?"

Why couldn't the flower cycle to meet his Valentine?

Because he lost his petals.

How do oak trees show their love for each other on Valentine's Day?

"I will never leaf you."

What did the tree say to his girlfriend on Valentine's Day?

Nothing. Trees can't talk!

Why was the cactus sad on Valentine's Day?

Because it was alone in the desert with nobody to love.

How did the herb ask his girlfriend on a date on Valentine's Day?

"I'd love to spend more thyme with you."

What did the bee say to the flower on Valentine's Day?

"Hi, honey!"

What did the flower say to his Valentine's date after making a joke?

"It wasn't serious; I was just pollen your leg."

What did the mountain say to her date on Valentine's Day?

"You are just hill-arious."

♥--♥--♥--♥--♥--▶

What candy did the Christmas tree give to his Valentine?

He gave her Orna-mints.

♥--♥--♥--♥--♥--▶

What kind of flowers shouldn't you gift your girlfriend?

Cauliflowers.

♥--♥--♥--♥--♥--▶

What did the cactus say to her Valentine's date when he arrived?"

"Wow, you're looking sharp!"

What do you call a tree nervous about his Valentine's date?

A sweaty palms.

How did the flower kiss his Valentine hello?

He used tulips.

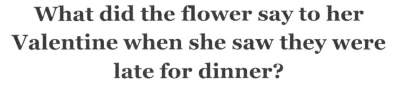

What did the flower say to her Valentine when she saw they were late for dinner?

"Put the petal on the metal!"

Why did the purple flower break up with her boyfriend on Valentine's Day?

She saw he had a violet streak.

CHAPTER 9
Tune In for These Valentine's Day Jokes

Why didn't the musician give his girlfriend balloons on Valentine's Day?

Because she hates pop music.

♥ - - ♥ - - ♥ - - ♥ - - ♥ - - ➤

Why was the singer's Valentine's Day surprise so special?

It hit all the right notes!

What instrument did the cucumber play for his girlfriend on Valentine's Day?

A pickle-o.

What concerts do frogs go to on Valentine's Day?

Hip-hop shows.

Why couldn't the athlete play any love songs on Valentine's Day?

Because he broke the record.

What instrument did the skeleton play for his Valentine's Day date?

The trom-bone.

How do guitarists ask their girlfriends on Valentine's Day dates?

"I pick you."

❤- -❤- -❤- -❤- -❤- -▶

What is a cat's favorite way to spend Valentine's Day?

Listening to mew-sic.

❤- -❤- -❤- -❤- -❤- -▶

Why didn't the cows go to a music concert on Valentine's Day?

Because there were no real moo-sicians.

What concert did the diamonds go watch on Valentine's Day?

A rock concert.

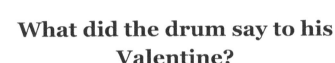

What did the drum say to his Valentine?

"My heart beats for you!"

What music concert did the mummies go to on Valentine's Day?

A rap concert.

Why did the hummingbird hum to his Valentine's date?

He forgot the words to the song.

What music do robots love to listen to on Valentine's Day?

Heavy metal.

How did the sun play romantic music on Valentine's Day?

He simply put on the ray-dio.

Why couldn't the piano keys go to the bar on Valentine's Day?

Because the bar wouldn't serve minors.

How did the pirate show his love for his Valentine?

He played her the guit-arrrrr.

What music did the needle play for the balloon on Valentine's Day?

Pop.

❤ - - ❤ - - ❤ - - ❤ - - ❤ - - ➤

What happened when the music teacher was late for her Valentine's Date?

She was in treble.

❤ - - ❤ - - ❤ - - ❤ - - ❤ - - ➤

Why couldn't the piano make it to his Valentine's Day date?

He left his keys inside.

❤ - - ❤ - - ❤ - - ❤ - - ❤ - - ➤

Why did the teenager put his radio in the fridge on Valentine's Day?

He wanted to play some cool music for his date.

Why couldn't the skeleton sing his Valentine a love song?

Because he had no guts.

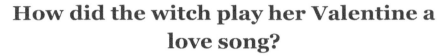

How did the witch play her Valentine a love song?

She just put on her broom-box.

Why did the chicken take his girlfriend to a music class on Valentine's Day?

They could join the band since they already had drumsticks.

Where did the bath sponge take his girlfriend on Valentine's Day?

To a soap-opera.

In what key did the cow sing to his Valentine?

In Beef-flat.

Why was the fish able to play his Valentine a song on the piano?

Because he knew all his scales.

What do the planets love to do on Valentine's Day?

They put the radio on and listen to Nep-tunes.

How did the triangle end his date with his Valentine?

"Thank you for every ting. See you next time."

How do musicians ask each other out on Valentine's Day?

Without you, my life would b-flat."

Why did the pirate sing to his girlfriend on Valentine's Day?

Because he was always able to reach the high C's.

Why did the grandparents put wheels on their rocking chairs on Valentine's Day?

They wanted to rock and roll.

CHAPTER 10
Toy-rific Valentine's Day Jokes

Why did the lego break up with each other on Valentine's Day?

Because they didn't fit together.

◆ - - ❤ - - ❤ - - ❤ - - ❤ - - ▶

Why was the teddy bear happy on Valentine's Day?

Because it was stuffed with love.

What did the toy soldier say to its Valentine?

"I'll always march to the beat of your heart."

What did the rubber duck say to his Valentine?

"You really quack me up!"

How did Rudolf know it was Valentine's Day?

He looked in his calen-deer.

Why didn't the monopoly money go on a Valentine's Date?

Because it had more cents than that.

What did the toy hammer get her boyfriend for Valentine's Day?

A pound cake.

❤ - - ❤ - - ❤ - - ❤ - - ❤ - - ➤

What happened when Elsa's boyfriend gave her a balloon on Valentine's Day?

She let it go.

❤ - - ❤ - - ❤ - - ❤ - - ❤ - - ➤

What did the stuffed tiger toy say to his Valentine?

"I am wild about you."

What did the lion-toy say to his Valentine?

"You are roar-some!"

Why wasn't the toy robot nervous about his Valentine's date?

Because he had nerves of steel.

Why couldn't the bike attend his Valentine's Day dinner?

He was two-tired.

How did the stuffed squirrel get his Valentine to like him?

He acted like a nut.

Why didn't the toy skeleton go out on Valentine's Day?

Because he had no body to go on a date with.

What did Barbie say to Ken on Valentine's Day?

"I'm doll-ighted to be yours!"

Why couldn't the teddy bear eat her Valentine's Day chocolates?

Because she was stuffed.

Why did the toy car give his girlfriend wheels for Valentine's Day?

He wanted to show her the fastest way to his heart.

What did the sandcastle say when his girlfriend asked him to be her Valentine?

"Shore."

Why was the toy car sad on Valentine's Day?

Because it didn't have anyone to take on a joy ride.

What did the toy boat say to his Valentine?

"I really want to start a row-mance!"

Why did the computer game break up with his Valentine?

Because she wasn't his type.

Why did the toy dinosaur give his girlfriend an explosive gift on Valentine's Day?

Because he wanted to show her, she was dino-mite.

What did the toy bird say to his girlfriend?

"You are a tweet."

What did the toy fish say to her boyfriend on Valentine's Day?

"You are quite a catch."

Why did the spider send his girlfriend a gift on Valentine's Day?

He was caught in a web of love.

Why did the giraffe's boyfriend walk out on their Valentine's Day date?

Because she was too high maintenance.

Why was the toy airplane alone on Valentine's Day?

He couldn't find a wingman.

Why couldn't the tyrannosaurus attend his Valentine's Dinner?

Because he's extinct.

Why couldn't the toy pony sing her Valentine a love song?

She was a little horse.

Why did the toy cow give his girlfriend flowers on Valentine's Day?

He wanted to show her he was udder-ly in love with her.

Why did the toy rabbit cancel his Valentine's dinner?

He was having a bad hare day.

Why didn't the boomerang go back to his Valentine?

It was just a stick.

What did the rubber duck say when his date wanted more gifts on Valentine's Day?

"Just put it on my bill."

CONGRATULATIONS!

Well, that's it for our Valentine's Day Joke Book for Kids! We hope you've had a great time reading and sharing these jokes with your friends and family. Remember, laughter is the best medicine, and nothing brings people together like a good laugh. So keep these jokes handy, and use them to brighten up someone's day.

If you've enjoyed this book, please leave a positive review on Amazon. We'd really appreciate it!

"The greatest thing you'll ever learn is to love and be loved in return."

NAT KING COLE

Made in the USA
Middletown, DE
03 February 2023

23843208R00064